# I loved you,

EVEN BEFORE YOU WERE BORN!

Caron Swensen Bear

**FriesenPress**

Suite 300 - 990 Fort St
Victoria, BC, V8V 3K2
Canada

www.friesenpress.com

**Copyright © 2017 by Swensen Press**
First Edition — 2017

ISBN
978-1-5255-0568-3 (Hardcover)
978-1-5255-0545-4 (Paperback)
978-1-5255-0546-1 (eBook)

*1. JUVENILE NONFICTION, FAMILY*

Distributed to the trade by The Ingram Book Company

I have had many careers, but being the mother to my four children, Sara, Katelyn, Travis and Joshua, has been the most rewarding and fulfilling thing I have ever done. And now I have been gifted with the opportunity to become a grandmother, which was my inspiration for writing this book. When your children become parents, it completes a beautiful and loving circle. I can hardly find the words to describe what a wonderful feeling it is to become a grandmother!

Dedicated to all my grandchildren, even before you were born!
Love, Grandma
July 14, 2016

*I would like to thank my kids for all their support, and
Travis, thank you for your confidence in me.*

Illustrations by D. Dana Robinson
Watercolors by Katelyn Bear

*I loved you,*
*even before you*
*were born!*

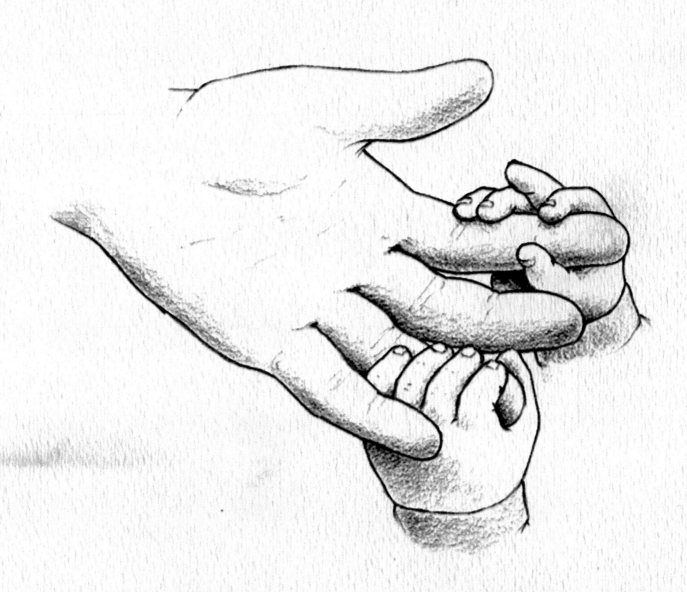

*I loved your tiny hands and couldn't wait to hold them.*

I loved your little feet and couldn't wait to kiss them.

I loved your sweet smiles and couldn't wait to see them.

I loved your soft coos and couldn't wait to hear them.

*I couldn't wait to watch you sleep.*

Oh, I could hardly wait to meet you!

And now that
you are here,
I love you even
MORE than before
you were born!

Now *I* get to hold your tiny hands and kiss your little feet!

*I* get to see your
sweet smiles
and hear your
soft coos!

*I get to watch you sleeping peacefully.*

I get to love you every day, even more than before you were born!

CPSIA information can be obtained
at www.ICGtesting.com
Printed in the USA
LVOW06*1915050717
540357LV00025B/504/P